AFFLICTION OF RACISM

A STUDY OF JAMES BALDWIN'S "GO TELL IT TO THE MOUNTAIN" AND "GIOVANNI'S ROOM"

DR P SUGANYA

Copyright © Dr P Suganya
All Rights Reserved.

ISBN 979-888569343-1

Contents

Foreword

In the late 1960 and early 1970 literary studies developed with a new approach called ethnicity and race. Blacks were discriminated against by Whites in all the categories such aseducation,employment, accommodation, medical care and unfairness in the criminal justice system. Race became a dividing line which made African Americans struggle a lot to get their rights of life, freedom, and happiness. It also spoiled the lives and safety of African Americans during this period. Baldwin has acknowledged the same in his novels Go Tell It on the Mountain, a semi-autobiographical novel and Giovanni's Room.

This book enumerates how Baldwin has described the lifestyle of white people and black people through his novels Go Tell It on the Mountain and Giovanni's Room. Through the settings of these novels, Baldwin has also projected the discrimination of the white and black people. Even, it analyses Baldwin's comparison of the dirty places as black people's places and gorgeous places as white people's places. It also highlights the symbolic representation used by Baldwin represents the discrimination and suffering of black people.

CHAPTER ONE

AFFLICTION OF RACISM

Racism is the domination and discrimination of one race over another race and prejudice takes results towards the people based on their race. Racism cannot be explained in a single word or a sentence because it is like an incurable disease spread throughout America. The overall ideology of racism consists of the people whom themselves segregated the particular group of people with their social behaviour and innate capacities and it can rank as inferior or superior. Historical examples of institutional racism include the Holocaust, the apartheid regime in South Africa, slavery and segregation in the United States, and slavery in Latin America were the historical examples of institutional racism. Many States and Empires have racism as one aspect of the social organisation.

Racism shows the superiority of one race over another and due to the race system the minority people suffered a lot, they were discriminated against by the majority people in all the criteria. In some cases, they have been treated like a slave and discriminated against on the basis of their family background and mode of dress. It happened because of the prejudgment of people, which made them hate if there were any discrepancies in the expectation.

Racism exists until the human being exists in the world. It might be defined as the hatred of one person by another or by denoting their life or status and the classification of the superior and inferior people. It classifies the people by noticing their skin colour, language, customs and place of birth or the factors which reveal the nature of the particular person or group. This classification among the people rose to the wars, slavery, the formation of nations and legal codes.

As Montgomery Jr. opined in American History, "RACISM IS AND ALWAYS HAS BEEN A FACT OF LIFE FOR African Americans. Over the centuries, many objects have been produced that reflect racist feelings, attitudes, and motivations" (249). During the past 500-1000 years, racism has been happening between Western people. The Western people do not accept the non-western people and they were separated and discriminated against. The most notable situation in the racism was the enslavement of Africans in the New World. This enslavement was accomplished because of the less population of Black Africans while Whites in large number with their descents.

There were different aspects of racism that become manifested in man's life and in society. Such as, Aversive racism was racism in which the persons behave sceptically by losing their consciousness to the negative thought as opposing others race, tradition, and cultural behaviour. Cultural racism exists where racism can be characterised when the superior people were dominated or neglected by the minority people by seeing their cultural behaviour. Racial discrimination refers to discrimination against some races which seems to be an inferior race.

Racial Segregation was the separation of people who have been separated by their racial group. Other than this there were several aspects of racism and Baldwin has used some of these aspects in his works, which is going to be the thematic study of this thesis. As John mentioned,"At their most intense, these race-war combats always transmute into sex combats – which illustrates Baldwin's theory of fundamentally sexual character of racism. This aspect of the novel, however, is even more unsettled and unsettling, because of the case Baldwin is trying to make for inversion" (42).

There were different characteristics of racism collectables, such as un-factual the first and foremost one, does not reveal the actual situation of African Americans and what they have created or produced or lived through. Second racism collectables are designed to justify the racist reaction, portraying blacks as inferior people and justifying the punishment given to them by denoting their situation and inferior position. Third, the collectors of racist do not take extra effect to collect the data of African Americans and sometimes they do miss some valuable and important history of African Americans.

Racism refers to the difference between the two groups of races likewise there is one more theme called Sexism, which differs between the two groups of Sex or Gender to show their superiority. Sexism means based on prejudice or discrimination based on sex or gender, discrimination is a belief that exhibits men are always superior to women no matter how capable she is. Sexism discriminates against the female gender in the entire category where males stepped ahead in power and domination. The oppression or discrimination is there in all the fields like economic, political, social or cultural.

Racism indicates the beliefs in the superiority, inferiority and spotlessness of a race which is based on the variation of the moral and intellectual characteristics. Racism is also a hatred of one group to another group due to the variation of their skin colour, language, culture and place of birth. Racist has categorised the particular race as superior and inferior on the basis of the immigration of the non-native people. It results in racial discrimination and racial arrogance. Racial discrimination singles out the discrimination made betwixt inferior and superior people based on their race. Racial arrogance was an illegal treatment of a certain group of people by denoting the race and culture of another group of people where they did not have any rights to do.

Racism happened in different places in different kinds of situations due to the skin colour, nationality, and background of the people and it leads to racial discrimination. As it was stated in, *Contemporary Racial Attitudes, Black and White: Their Social and Psychological Implications* that:

Based upon approximately 2,500 respondents in fifteen cities throughout the United States, the data explore the feeling of whites towards blacks on a variety of subjects, including governmental policy toward blacks. It will come as little surprise to the reader that significant disparities exist between blacks and whites in their perceptions of social reality. (51)

People were humiliated and did not have equal freedom or opportunities due to racial discrimination, only the seniority group of people got all the opportunities even though they were not capable of it and the minority group of people was excluded from all sorts of activities. Racism is exposed through the behaviour of the people towards the minority people. Sometimes it was confessed in the systems and organisations. It was the culmination of the barricade that stops the minority people to lead their life to their expectations.

Racism has been experienced by lots of people, it happened all over the world. It is experienced mostly in places like workplaces, nearby homes, and public places. The minority people would not get proper recognition even though they work properly and superior people would get all the publicity. Even in the play, blacks would enact only the minor role like office boy, waiter, and cleaner, they did not get leading roles which add weightage to their career. Likewise, the first priority would be given to the white people in the interview and then to the black people. It was difficult to get seats for black people even in educational institutions.

Racism is not the inbuilt quality of people, it has been cultivated in their brought up. It might be the misconception of the superiority towards minority people. As Hughes quoted from *Notes of a Native Son*, ". . . his birthright as a man no less than his birthright as a black man, . . ." (21). However, racism was not only out of hatred, some were out of fear and unpleasant emotions. Some may happen due to the ignorance and innocence of the people. It is dangerous to individuals, communities and society at large. Though racism leads to the suppression of certain category people and they would get frustrated due to it. Even, it also leads to depression, it would force them to take the wrong decisions in life. As Collier mentioned, "It is this blindness on the part of Euro-Americans which has created and perpetuated the vicious racism which threatens to destroy this nation" (33).

Racism was a kind of disease that started when human beings started their life. It was initiated from slavery, in the ancient period the places have been conquered by other country people and the people who captured the land made the native people a slave. Those people have been sold and bought as slaves to work for other countries. The people who have been enslaved got freedom from slavery later and led their lives in the same country. Automatically, they would be different from the native people's behaviour, skin colour and culture, and from there racism emerged. Racism and other forms of discrimination led to Civil War and due to racism, trillions of Jews were assassinated in World War II by Hitler and he gave an explanation to Hermann Rouschning that:

'I know perfectly well,' 'he said, just as well as all these tremendously clever intellectuals, that in the scientific sense there is no such thing as race. . . . And I was a politician need a conception which enables the order which has hitherto existed on historic bases to be abolished and an entirely new and antihistorical order enforced and given an intellectual basis . . . . With the conception of race, National Socialism will carry its revolution abroad and recast the world'. (Bayne).

Even other countries including the United States have followed the same racist techniques to get a victory in the war.

Racism was practised in different structures in America from the ancient era. The American people started to capture other countries step by step. Similarly, they captured India, unknowingly Indians turned into prisoners by themselves in their own land. Meanwhile, other countries like Mexican, Filipino, and Puerto Ricans were captured by the whites and the Americans created a belief that other skin colours were inferior to them other than white colour. As a critic stated in *The Gilder Lehrman Center for the Study of Slavery, Resistance, and Abolition*:

Although a citizen of the United States, the black man is regarded by the white American as an inferior being . . ."Accordingly, racism evolved in America and later on, it becomes a part of American law. Then the people started to sobriquet the other country people as "You can't trust a Jew", "Niggers are shiftless", and "Don't give an Indian whiskey; he'll go crazy".

Racism was not materialised from birth, it was accomplished from the parents, elders, neighbours, and friends indulged in racism. If there were any changes in the law related to racism automatically the people would change their mentality towards racism. But the government passed the law only according to the people's behaviour, if the people opposed racism and other discrimination definitely the government tries to wipe out racism from the country.

African Americans were always under racism directly or indirectly and they were always treated inferior. Their hard work would not be shown out at any cost, whatever the black people created or produced it would be released by white people in a different name. Racists opposed the black people as ignorant and foolish and they did not appoint black people in an administration or in an important position in the institutions or organisations. There were many themes framed by racists about black people, as stated by Montgomery Jr., that,

Blacks are intellectually inferior, unintelligent and simple-minded; Blacks were born to be slaves or servants and should not aspire to be at the same social and economic level as whites; Blacks are happy with a low station and a meagre lot in life and need or want little else; Blacks are morally inferior and given to crime and various forms of dishonesty; Black speech (Negro dialect) and culture should be ridiculed; the physical features of Blacks are ugly and strange; Blacks do and believe things that are ridiculous, superstitious, and laughable; Blacks have and should be called various derogatory names, which are fun to use; Blacks are subhuman and at the same level as animals; Blacks are associated with subservient menial occupations" (cooking, domestic, service, and unskilled labour); Blacks are good at entertaining others but have few other skills and little else to think about. (250)

To create awareness against racism, the writers began to expose the problems of black people in America. It was also done by American and African American writers like Maya Angelou, Richard Wright, Butler, and W.E.B. Du Bois. All these writers have discussed the problems of race and racism in their works and even some of the African American Writers have faced racism personally in their life. Among those writers, Baldwin was one of the most famous and important writers who faced racist issues in his own life. Henceforth, he has focused on issues of racism in most of his works which seem to be an eye-opener for the people.

James Arthur Baldwin was an American Novelist, essayist, story writer, dramatist, poet, scriptwriter, author of children's books and a non-fiction writer. In the Twentieth Century African American Literature, Baldwin was recognised as one of the important writers. His works consist of racism and sexism in American Society and challenge the readers to find out the differences between race and sex. During the period of the Civil Rights Movement, he was recommended as a leading literary spokesperson by many people, due to that he became too popular and reached the highest position in the literary field. His writings depict the sufferings and difficulties of the African Americans and it acted like a universal symbol of human conflict. As Terry opined from Achebe's speech:

He said of Jimmy Baldwin, "Baldwin wants to lift from the backs of Black people the burden of their race" and that he "wrestled to unmask the face of his oppressor, to see his face and to call him by name." James Baldwin said to us, "Go back to where you started or as far back as you can. Examine all of it. Travel your road again and tell the truth about it. Sing or shout or testify or keep it to yourself, but know whence you came." (62)

Baldwin was considered to be one of the most prestigious writers in African American literature. He exposed the racial and sexual polarization of American society in his first and famous novel *Go Tell It on the Mountain*. In the 1960s, he was regarded by many as the leading literary spokesperson of the Civil Rights Movement and he became popular. His novels, essays, and other works vouch for his arguments that the black American, as an object of suffering and abuse, represents a universal symbol of human conflict. His works mostly focus on the set of themes such as race, racism and effects of skin colour on a social group which also tells about the social, religious and material experience of the group.

Baldwin, African American writer has used racism as a central theme in most of his works and he was a successful black writer during his era. As a black person, he could analyse and focus on the sufferings and problems of black people. To escape from the racism he shifted his place to Paris and there he met Richard Wright, with his support he published his first novel. As Thornton pointed out, ". . .

James Baldwin in "Stranger in the Village" recognized that the African American slave . . ." (733). He has depicted how black people have been suffered due to racism and how white people discriminated the black people.

Baldwin's first novel was *Go Tell It on the Mountain*, it has been divided into three parts, Part I-'The Seventh Day', Part II-'The Prayers of Saints' and it has been subdivided into three, such as 'Florence's Prayer', 'Gabriel's Prayer' and 'Elizabeth's Prayer' and Part III-'The Threshing-Floor'. All three parts of this novel expose the inner feelings of all the characters in this novel. It delivered the lifestyle and sufferings of the African American people and their relationship with their families. It mainly focused on the racism, rituals of Christianity, Prayer and Church. It also depicted sex, violence and death. Death has been taken place in the few parts of the novel due to disillusionment and social issues faced by the characters.

Go Tell It on the Mountain was a semi-autobiographical novel by Baldwin. It depicted the life and experience of the author. The novel begins by showing the chief protagonist John Grimes who played the role of Baldwin. John was black in his appearance and his family name Grimes, means dirt, it represents blackness which followed him throughout his life. He woke up from his sleep on Saturday which was his fourteenth birthday, but no one remembered his birthday including his mother. That exhibited the negligence of a person in a family and his depression emerged from the very moment onwards. The family members were getting ready for the church, at that time he was thinking about the past memories. There was a swap of past and present in the whole novel. In the flashback, he was thinking about a day when he and his half-brother Roy were on their way to the church named Temple of the Fire-

Baptized at Harlem.

On the way to church, he could observe the local people shouting and fighting at each other and they were shabby in their appearance. The people were shouting, laughing and using rubbish words in the street. That depicted the culture and behaviour of the black people which makes others scare by seeing them, "John and Roy, passing these men and women, looked at one another briefly, John embarrassed and Roy amused. Roy would be like them when he grew up if the Lord did not change his heart" (GTM 12). There was a great confusion that, the African American's lifestyle changed because of their behaviour or the racial discrimination changed their behaviour.

The novel moved on to the present situation, John's mother assigned work for him in spite of his birthday by denoting his father, Gabriel Grimes. Grimes' family was under the control of Gabriel Grimes, step-father of John Grimes. At the earlier stage of the novel, Gabriel treated John inferiorly and he showed partiality between his stepson John and his own son Roy, like black and white discrimination. This inferiority complex made John worry a lot, even though, he would obey whatever Gabriel says but Roy would not obey and sometimes he used to oppose his father. Baldwin has compared this discrimination with the black and white discrimination and in that particular scene, John's father Gabriel has been portrayed as a white man in the black image. As Bhattacharya stated that:

John receives his first lessons of hatred in his own family from a father who accepted the white image of black man's inferiority that found frequent expressions in his anger and in his clinching to religions as his only redemption from the sorry state of things and does not reciprocate John's love for him, and the latter ascribes this to his ugliness and blackness while making attempts to get rid of the stigma that gives him rejection. (17)

John was doing cleaning work assigned by his mother at the same time he was observing the children playing on the street and he was longing too much for it. It shows that he does not have enough freedom to fulfil his wishes in his life, though he was a black boy he was continuously warned by his stepfather Gabriel to be careful with the white people. There was an incident that happened when John was in his school, he felt sick due to a cold and he was taken care of by a teacher by providing cod-liver oil, she also prepared special syrup for him to drink. It made his mother appreciate the teacher but his father's opinion was totally contrasted to their opinion. John could remember the statement of his stepfather about white people that:

His father said that all white people were wicked and that God was going to bring them low. He said that white people were never to be trusted, that they told nothing but lies, and that not one of them had ever loved a nigger. He, John, was a nigger, and he would find out, as soon as he got a little older, how evil white people could be. John had read about the things white people did to coloured people; how, in the South, where his parents came from, white people cheated them of their wages, and burned them, and shot them – and did worse things, said his father, which the tongue could not endure to utter. He had read about coloured men being burned in the electric chair for things they had not done; how in riots they were beaten with clubs; how they were tortured in prisons; how they were the last to be hired and the first to be fired. (GTM 41-42)

John was aware of his father's warning, that black people should not believe white people. According to the coloured people, the white was always wicked and they would not trust them at any cost. But Roy, his half-brother did not listen to his father's warning and often goes to the street to play with white boys. One day he was hurt by white boys, there was no clear picture of the incident but his father accused white people and he too blamed John and his mother who failed to take care of Roy. As it was stated, "'You come here, boy,' he said, 'and see what them white folks done to your brother.' (GTM 52) 'It was white folks, some of the white folks *you* like so much that tried to cut your brother's throat'" (GTM 53).

Black people were frightened by observing the culture and behaviour of the white people because black people's lifestyle was totally different compared to white people. John on his birthday went to Central Park with permission and money given by his mother for his birthday. Central Park was a place dominated by white people, there he got stunned by observing the behaviour of the white people and according to him and his father, white people were committing sin. The lifestyle of white people made John isolated in that area. He hesitated to enter the library and theatre which seemed to be an irrelevant place for him, "And then everyone, all the white people inside, would know that he was not used to great buildings, or too many books, and they would look at him with pity" (GTM 42-43). It described that colour people were totally different and they were not used to great buildings and books, all were restricted to them due to their skin colour. Even their equality has been barricaded by the white people and the black people were treated inferior to the white people.

Baldwin has used symbolic representation as "dust and dirt" in this novel. In the first phase of the novel, John was thinking about the day he goes to Church with Roy. He observed the black people in the street and they seemed to be, ". . . wrinkled and dusty now, muddy-eyed and muddy-faced;" (GTM 12). Then John was asked to clean his mother's room at his house which was full of "dust and dirt". While he was cleaning it the dust and dirt circulated him, ". . . dust rose, clogging his nose and sticking to his sweaty skin, . . . the clouds of dust would not diminish, the rug would not be clean" (GTM 29). Then in the next scene, he has gone to clean the Church, it was full of "dust and dirt" like his mother's room and he felt that, "The darkness and silence of the church pressed on him, cold as judgment, and the voices crying from the window might have been crying from another world" (GTM 57).

All the above three incidents represented the "dust and dirt" of the places. Baldwin has used this symbolic representation as black people's life, their life was filled with "dust and dirt" like white people surrounded the black people. However, the black people tried to wipe out the dust, to get purified but they couldn't. Eventually, darkness would not go off from black people's life like how the Church was in darkness and the black people would always hear the voice of racism across the world. As Bhattacharya opined, "John on careful observation finds filth, dirt and darkness-a symbol of evil and degradation - pervading his home and the Harlem Ghetto" (17).

Part II- 'The Prayers of the Saints' in *Go Tell It on the Mountain*, was dealt with the prayer of Florence, Gabriel, and Elizabeth in the Church. That part was divided into three and each of the divisions brings out the flashback and the earlier lifestyle, sufferings and problems faced due to racism. The first division was Florence's Prayer, John's aunt, it described the obstacle of her earlier life. It depicted the family bonding and how it got collapsed when she tried to come out from racial problems. Baldwin has covered it mostly on racism, slavery, and sexual harassment of the white people to black people and it has also focused on gender discrimination.

Florence's mother was a slave while Florence was a child and her mother lost her husband and children due to slavery at that time, only Florence and Gabriel were remaining out of all the children. Florence was also thinking about white domination during her mother's period while she was young. The people stand motionless while the white people come for rounds, "Silence filled the room after her 'Amen,' and in the silence they heard, far up the road, the sound of a horse's hoofs" (GTM 77). The black people would be silent, they turn off the lamps, stay still if they hear the sound of white people's horse hoofs sound to safeguard their family and children from white people. Because, if the white people see any black girl while they were coming they would drag the girl to the field to fulfil their pleasures. It happened to Deborah, Florence's neighbourhood who was three years older than Florence and she has been raped by white people brutally.

In nineteen hundred, when Florence was twenty-six, she was working as a servant maid and cook in the white family. One day she was treated badly by the white man, so she quit the job and decided to move on to New York to lead her life. The black people particularly the black girls did not have any safety and they would not get a proper job to lead their life due to racial problems. As it was mentioned, "She had been working as cook and serving-girl for a large white family in town, and it was on the day her master proposed that she become his concubine that she knew her life among these wretched people had come to its destined end" (GTM 85). But none of her family members allowed her to go out to lead her life up to her wish. They tried to convince her but she did not hear their wordings and at last, by thinking of the partiality shown by her mother between Florence and Gabriel, she left her family. Finally, she moved from her home to escape from racism and to get deliverance. Hence, to escape from the discrimination and suppression the black people were ready to leave their birthplace too.

Gabriel's Prayer was about the past memories of his life and his relationship with the girls. He committed lots of sin while he was young but at last, he became a preacher. He realised his mistakes only at the time of his mother's final stage of her deathbed and he practised as a preacher after her death. After his mother's death, he has taken care of by Deborah, his neighbour and he decided to marry her. Deborah encouraged Gabriel to preach at Twenty-Four Elders Revival Meeting and with the help of Deborah, he shined as a preacher.

One day while he has gone to a pharmacy to get medicine for Deborah, a group of white people was standing at the corner of that place. Gabriel hesitated to cross a group of white people since he was a preacher, white people left him free otherwise they would have killed him. As it was described:

. . . white men stood in groups of half-a-dozen. As he passed each group, silence fell, and they watched him insolently, itching to kill; but he said nothing, bowing his head, and they knew, anyway, that he was a preacher. There were no black men on the streets at all, save him. There had been found that morning, just outside of town, the dead body of a soldier, his uniform shredded where he had been flogged, and, turned upward through the black skin, raw, red meat. (GTM 164)

The above statement signifies that white people tend to kill black people just because they crossed them. Black people feel unsafe even to cross white people because white people would kill black people without any mercy. Black people do not have equal freedom even to walk in the street, they hesitate to walk in the street if the white people are in that place. The black people were not enjoying the minimum freedom even to walk in the street.

Black people suffered a lot due to white people's behaviour and torture. The white people often attack black people and sometimes it goes to the extreme level by killing the black people. Due to the unbearable torture by the white people, the black people's inner thoughts were fully filled with vengeance against white people. Likewise, the black people could defeat the white people only in their dream, not in real life, "yet he dreamed of the feel of a white man's forehead against his shoe; again and again, until the head wobbled on the broken neck and his foot encountered nothing but the rushing blood" (GTM 164). The black people used to curse the white people because they could not tolerate the torture of white people. So, black people used to curse the white people by stating that, "the big house, house of pride where the white folks lived, would come down; it was written in the Word of God" (GTM 79).

Baldwin relates Gabriel's sexual events with racism. When Gabriel decided to get married Deborah, who was brutally raped by white people and still her whole body fills with white man's milk, "She had been choked so early on white men's milk, and it remained so sour in her belly yet, that she would never be able, now, to find a nigger who would let her taste his richer, sweeter substances" (GTM 123). So, to rescue Deborah from that racial brutal suffering, to make her royal and to forget the harassment that happened to her, Gabriel married her. Likewise, when he had a sexual relationship with Esther he thinks about the place of the white man. Esther and Gabriel had a sexual relationship at the white man's house in the kitchen and while Esther revealed her pregnancy to Gabriel they were in the White man's yard. It frightened him a lot by thinking about the white people, if they come to know about the secret relationship with them it would lead to a different problem. This substantiates that while Gabriel thinks about Deborah, White People's brutal behaviour could be seen in his eyes similarly when he thinks about Esther he could feel the same fear by thinking white people. As Powers proclaimed, "For Gabriel, the desires of his body threaten to undermine his gimmick. Indeed, race plays a role in nearly every major sexual event of Gabriel's life" (800). Whenever Gabriel wants to fulfil his desire he experienced racial encounters.

Gabriel migrated his place from rural South to Harlem city, the change of the place changed his character as well as his behaviour. While Gabriel was in the rural South he committed lots of sin and he ran behind the lust. Moreover, while he was in Harlem, he took care of his family and tried to safeguard his children including his stepson John from the white people. That represents the drastic change in his life and through Gabriel's change over in his life, Baldwin has represented Black masculine responsibility and race leadership.

Elizabeth's Prayer denoted racial discrimination due to skin colour. Elizabeth was a colour girl, the daughter of a "very fair and beautiful" (GTM 177) mother and a black father. Due to her skin colour, her biological mother did not show enough affection to her, "Her mother did not, however, hold Elizabeth in her arms very often. Elizabeth very quickly suspected that this was because she was so very much darker than her mother and not nearly, of course, so beautiful" (GTM 177). That affected Elizabeth a lot, while she has gone to kiss her mother, her mother moved away from her by thinking of it as an unpleasant movement and she avoided Elizabeth all the time. Her father, who resembled her, has taken care of Elizabeth and showed affection towards her. This scene exposed skin colour discrimination. Even her own mother was not accepting her due to her skin colour and her mother used to mention Elizabeth as an "unnatural child". There should not be any variation to show affection to their own children but here the skin colour differences made the African American people distinguish the affection towards their own children.

Elizabeth after her mother's death was forced to move to her aunt's house and there she fell in love with a coloured boy named, Richard. Elizabeth and Richard decided to move to the North so that they could earn more money and could lead their life happily. Both have moved to the North, there during the daytime, they both were working in the store and in the night, Richard used to go to school. Wherever they have gone, Richard used to explain and give historical details about the places and situations. Elizabeth wondered by observing his knowledge and asked him the reason. He came out with the reason that, "'I just decided me one day that I was going to get to know everything them white bastards knew, and I was going to get to know it better than them, so could no white son-of-a-bitch *nowhere* talk *me* down, and never make me feel like *I* was dirt, when I could read him the alphabet, back, front, sideways" (GTM 194).

The above quotes cleared that the colour people were not allowed to educate properly and they were not aware of the places in their own country. Black people did not have equal rights to cultivate their knowledge, they were discriminated against due to race and colour even in the schools and institutions. The above quotes turned out that the colour people were improving themselves to be equal to white people's knowledge and they could use it as a tool to escape from racism. As Araselvi stated, "He read a lot and thought of liberty and equality" (173). If the black people get educated properly like white people they could escape from racism and it was also proved that there was racism even in the educational institutions. So, the only solution to avoid racism is to educate all the people equally without any discrimination.

Richard and Elizabeth were leading their life happily, one day Richard was arrested by the white policemen without proper reason. According to the white people and policemen, all the black people were criminals and they would not tell the reason for arresting black people. It happened in Richard's life that:

He was about to ask them what the trouble was when, running across the tracks towards them, and followed by a white man, he saw another coloured boy; and at the same instant another white man came running down the underground steps. Then he came fully awake, in panic; he knew that whatever the trouble was, it was now his trouble also; for these white men would make no distinction between him and the three boys they were after. (GTM 198)

The above statement gives a clear picture that, if one was culprit among the black people the white people used to accuse all the black people around that place and they would not believe the innocence of the black man who was not in a part of the crime. The white people would not believe black people even though they were with enough explanation. According to the white people, all the black people were culprits. As Richard voiced out, "He said at last that he would die before he signed a confession to something he hadn't done. 'Well then,' said one of them, hitting him suddenly across the head, 'maybe you *will* die, you black son-of-a-bitch'" (GTM 199). Hence, it was clear that black people did not have right to justify themselves.

Last part- The Threshing-Floor of the novel *Go Tell It on the Mountain*, described the whole situation that happened in the church. All were kneeling in front of God to get rid of sin and crying to the core by thinking that all the niggers have been cursed. As it was stated, "All niggers had been cursed, the ironic voice reminded him, all niggers had come from this most undutiful of Noah's sons" (GTM 228). That was the statement of John in the novel but it was the overall mindset of all the 'niggers' because they have been affected too much in the world due to racism. Wherever black people go they have been discriminated against and suppressed by all the white people

Hence, *Go Tell It on the Mountain* exposed the detailed life of black people and how they suffered due to the perception of white people. It described the story of black people separation, freedom, and equality. Black people have been separated from their families to come up in their life and they were also shifting the place from South to North to cultivate and educate themselves. Throughout the novel, Baldwin has shown the characters emote as Negros and their sufferings while they are kneeling in front of God. As Powers stated, "In different ways, the psychic and spiritual crises facing Gabriel and his stepson, John, announce a thematic of race, sexuality, and gender that occupied Baldwin throughout his career" (798). It also examined that black's life was a cursed life and God was their only hope and belief who would rescue them from this cursed world. *Go Tell It on the Mountain*, depicts that the people get relief from racism if they, go tell it to God.

Giovanni's Room was Baldwin's second novel and it was a problematic novel at that time. It was not like other novels of Baldwin. The other novels were mostly based on race and racism but this novel was fully focused on the Homosexual and Heterosexual relationship of the characters in this novel. Due to theme, the novel was rejected by Knopf publisher who published Baldwin's first novel. Then it was published by Dial publisher and later it was converted into a play. The problem behind the rejection was homosexuality. The whole novel focused on a homosexual relationship which was against the culture of Americans at that time, but Baldwin has focused on that in a different way.

Giovanni's Room was focused on David, the protagonist of this novel and his sexual relationship with other characters. He was indulged in both Homosexual and Heterosexual relationships. Homosexuality means having a sexual relationship with the same gender and Heterosexuality means having sexual relations with the opposite gender. Hence, this novel depicted the culmination of both the Homosexual and Heterosexual relationship. As Malarkodi affirmed that, "He takes up love in its various dimensions: Love between man and woman, man and man and between blacks and whites" (74). At the same time, it was focused on the problems faced by the sexual relationship which was totally absurd.

Most of the readers and critics have described the novel as a raceless novel but it was wrong. The novel also consisted of racism by comparing Homosexuality and Heterosexuality with black and white. Many critics have mentioned that Homosexuality depicts Blackness and Heterosexuality depicts Whiteness, as Armengol mentioned in the article, "More specifically, I will argue that in *Giovanni's Room*, as in *Another Country* (Baldwin [1962]1993), race is deflected onto sexuality with the result that whiteness is transvalued as heterosexuality, just as homosexuality becomes associated with blackness, both literally and metaphorically" (673).

As given in the above statement it has been verified that Heterosexuality represents white and Homosexuality represents black. White always denotes purity, good and neatness as it represents white people on the other hand black represents ugly, bad and untidy as it represents black people. So, here it can be considered that Heterosexuality represents white people and Homosexuality represents black people.

David, the protagonist of this novel had a Homosexual relationship with an Italian boy Giovanni and his childhood friend Joey and a Heterosexual relationship with Sue and Hella. As it was discussed in the previous paragraph, whenever Joey and Giovanni have been shown in the novel they have been represented something related to black and when Hella and Sue entered the scene they have been represented something related to white. Likewise, when Joey was shown first time, David was describing Joey as "dark" (GR 5) and Giovanni as "insolent, dark" (25) Sue was described as ". . . blonde, and rather puffy, with the quality, in spite of the fact . . ." (85) and Hella as ". . . her hair was a little shorter, and her face was tan, and she wore the same brilliant smile" (GR 106). These descriptions distinguished the black and white differences. Baldwin has used symbolic representations of racism in this novel like how Richard Wright has shown in his works.

Baldwin has portrayed the places in this novel to depict black people and racism. As per the general information quoted in the other novels of Baldwin, similarly, he has depicted "dust and dirt" as a symbolic representation of black people's skin colour. While Giovanni's room has been shown in the novel, the room seems to be ugly and dirty and the window was closed which depicted that the darkness should prevail in that room and light should not enter the room. Eventually, the room of Hella is portrayed as neat and clean with full of light which depicted white. Since Giovanni's room has been portrayed with dust and dirt because David and Giovanni had their homosexual relationship in that room which depicted blackness and in Hella's room it was a Heterosexual relationship with David which depicted whiteness. These were the symbolic representation used by Baldwin in this novel to depict racism.

Baldwin has used symbolic representation even at the end of the novel. Giovanni was represented as darkness and dirt at the climax of the novel when Giovanni was about to start his new journey by leaving this sinful world. The darkness and silence surrounded him, the jail in charge seemed to be dark, Giovanni's face seemed to be dark, and all this darkness, black, and dirt were taking him to begin his new journey. At the same time, David neglected Giovanni to lead his life with Hella and want to enjoy the white privileges but at last, he was thrown into the darkness of life by standing alone on the road. As Armengol pointed out, "David seeks not only to leave behind blackness and dirt but also to recover the privileges of whiteness and heterosexuality and, in so doing, preserve his manhood" (682-683).

According to the Americans, whites were always in a high position and blacks were in the lower position likewise the Heterosexuality was a decent relationship and it was not against American culture but Homosexuality was not like that it was totally contrasted to the former one, it makes the people be ashamed. Like how white people have all the freedom in America and Blacks did not have equal freedom and rights like white people. Likewise, David did not feel bad to have relationships with Sue and Hella but he felt guilty to have a relationship with Joey and Giovanni. As Bigsby opined, "For some of this reality is one's racial or sexual nature, for others, it is the ineluctable fact of death" (51). White people in America utilise black people for their needs and then neglect the black people, similarly, here David used Giovanni for his need and avoided him after Hella has come, as David exposed that, "I felt a great need to get out of there before Giovanni arrived" (GR 114).

Baldwin compared homosexuality with racism in this novel. According to his opinion, if the people did not frighten by seeing anything or doing anything, automatically it would get vanish. As well if the black people did not frighten by seeing white people, racism would get vanish. As Bigsby stated, "Baldwin says of homosexuality in America that "if people were not frightened of it . . . it really would cease in effect . . . to exist. I mean in the same way, the Negro problem would disappear," it is no accident that the two ideas should appear so closely related" (51-52).

Baldwin has depicted *Giovanni's Room* from a different perspective than other novels. Through the sexual relationships, he has depicted racism by portraying David with Giovanni, Joey, Hella, and Sue. He proved Racism through the descriptions of the characters, situations and places in the novel. As Armengol proclaimed, "I will be arguing that race and sexuality in Baldwin are not simply interrelated but virtually interchangeable so that homosexuality becomes, literally and metaphorically, associated with blackness at the same time that heterosexuality is, as we shall see, indissolubly linked to whiteness" (674). Hence, the novel *Giovanni's Room* disclosed the room of racism in this novel.

To conclude, this chapter brings out how Baldwin has projected racism in his novels and how it is reflected through the characters of the novels. The novels even described the experience and the real incidents which affected the African Americans. The African American novelists used to expose real-life incidents of the black people to portray the problems of the characters in the novels, which gave additional ingredients for the novels where other writers failed to inculcate in their works. Baldwin had a keen eye on each and every character and from life to death scenes of his novels to explore black's life by focusing on various concepts, denoting skin colour of black and white people as an important tool.

Reference:

Araselvi, M. Shamuna Jerrin. "Portrayal of women in James Baldwin's *Go Tell It on the Mountain." Contemporary Discourse*, Jan. 2014, pp. 172-74.

Armengol, Joseph M. "In the Dark Room: Homosexuality and / as Blackness in James Baldwin's Giovanni's Room." *Signs*, vol. 37, no. 3, Spring, 2012, pp. 671-693. *JSTOR*, www. jstor.org/stable/10.1086/662699.

Baldwin, James. *Giovanni's Room*. Penguin Books, United States Of America, 1956, pp. 1-150.

Baldwin, James. Go Tell It on the Mountain. Penguin Books, Great Britain, 1954, pp. 1-256.

Bayness, H.G. "The Source of Hitler's Ideas." *Germany Possessed*: *Psychology Revivals*. Routledge, 5 Aug. 2016, books.google.co.in/books?

Bhattacharya, Ajita. "The Church /Identity Dilemma in *Go Tell It On The Mountain*." *Littcrit*, June-Dec. 1999, pp. 13-22.

Collier, Eugenia. "Thematic Patterns in Baldwin's Essays." *Contemporary Literary Criticism*, edited by Riley, Carolyn and Barbara Harte, vol. 2, Gale, 1974, p. 33. *Originally Published in Black World*, June 1972, pp.28-34.

Hughes, Langston. "From Harlem to Paris." *Contemporary Literary Criticism*, edited by Gunton, Sharon R, vol. 17, Gale, 1981, p. 21. *Originally Published in The New York Times Review*,26Feb. 1956, p. 26.

Malarkodi, V. "Love-Hate Relationship in James Baldwin's Another Country." *The Rainbow*, Rajasekaran, G. and K. Rajaraman, Perambalur: Mercury Printers and Publishers, 2009, pp. 70-88.

McLeod, Saul. *Simply Psychology: Social Psychology.* 2007, www.simplypsychology.org/social-psychology.html.

Montgomery, Elvin, Jr., editor. "Racism." *A Celebration of America's Black Heritage Through Documents, Artifacts, and Collectibles: American History*, Chp. Vii, Stewart, Tabori and Chang, 2001, pp. 249-50.

Powers, Lyall H. "Henry James and James Baldwin: The Complex Figure." *Modern Fiction Studies*, Winter 1984, pp.

651-67.

Powers, Peter Kerry. "The Treacherous Body: Isolation, Confession, and Community in James Baldwin." *American Literature*, Dec. 2005, pp.787-814.

Terry, Esther. *Black Writers Redefine the Struggle: A Tribute to James Baldwin*. edited by Chametzky, Jules, Institute for Advanced Study in the Humanities, University of Massachusetts Press, 1989, pp. 62-81.

Thornton, Jerome E. "The Paradoxical Journey of the African American Fiction." *New Literary History*, vol.21, no. 3, Spring 1990, pp. 733-745. *JSTOR*, www. jstor.org/stable/ 469136.

www.ingramcontent.com/pod-product-compliance
Lightning Source LLC
Chambersburg PA
CBHW052136150726
48002CB00006B/2641